Facing Shadows

Facing Shadows

Ha Jin

Hanging Loose Press
Brooklyn, New York

Published by Hanging Loose Press, 231 Wyckoff Street, Brooklyn, New York 11217. All rights reserved. No part of this book may be reproduced without the publisher's written permission, except for brief quotations in reviews.

Printed in the United States of America

10 9 8 7 6 5 4 3 2

Hanging Loose Press thanks the Fund for Poetry and the Literature Programs of the National Endowment for the Arts and the New York State Council on the Arts for grants in support of this book's publication.

Acknowledgment is made to the following publications, where some of the poems in this book first appeared: *Agni*, "I Woke Up—Smiling," "My Mother Also Ate," "On a Pottery Figure of a Storyteller from the Eastern Han Dynasty"; *The Boston Phoenix*, "To My Grandmother Who Died Fourteen Years Ago in Manchuria"; *The Cresset*, "The Fight" and "Blessing"; *New England Review*, "The Past"; *Patagonian Winds*, "War"; *Ploughshares*, "A Child's Nature"; *Poetry*, "Ways of Talking"; *Shantih*, "Bargain"; *TriQuarterly*, "If You Have Not Thrown Me Away." "They Come" and "An Escape" appeared in *Out of the Howling Storm: The New Chinese Poetry*, ed. Tony Barnstone (Wesleyan University Press, 1993).

Art by Emily Cheng. Cover: *The Folds of Memory*, 38" x 33", oil/aluminum. Frontispiece: *Co-mingle*, 54" x 48", oil/linen.

Cover design by Caroline Drabik.

Library of Congress Cataloging-in-Publication Data

Jin, Ha
    Facing shadows / Ha Jin.
      p.   cm.
      ISBN 1-882413-25-3 (cloth). — ISBN 1-882413-24-5 (pbk.)
      1. Chinese Americans—Poetry.   I. Title.
PS3560.I6F3   1996
811'.54—dc20   95-49710
                        CIP

Produced at The Print Center, Inc., 225 Varick St., New York, NY 10014, a non-profit facility for literary and arts-related publications. (212) 206-8465

CONTENTS

1 Ways of Talking

2 They Come

3 At Midnight

4 Nets

For my teachers:
Allen Grossman & Frank Bidart

Ways of Talking

Ways of Talking

We used to like talking about grief.
Our journals and letters were packed
with losses, complaints, and sorrows.
Even if there was no grief
we wouldn't stop lamenting
as though longing for the charm
of a distressed face.

Then we couldn't help expressing grief.
So many things descended without warning:
labor wasted, loves lost, houses gone,
marriages broken, friends estranged,
ambitions worn away by immediate needs.
Words lined up in our throats
for a good whining.
Grief seemed like an endless river—
the only immortal flow of life.

[After losing a land and then giving up a tongue,
we stopped talking of grief.]
Smiles began to brighten our faces.
We laugh a lot, at our own mess.
Things become beautiful,
even hailstones in the strawberry fields.

*Once you lose everything, you realize how
good life was. = change in attitude.*

To My Grandmother Who Died in Manchuria Fourteen Years Ago

Grandma, is it dangerous to write to you?
Everybody told me to forget the dream
I had last night when you came home
and cooked us a Mid-Fall meal.
You even smiled at me when I swept
your room with a huge broom.
Before supper you gave me
a bowl of stewed meat and whispered,
"Save this for the kids when they need it."

I was shocked.
How could you speak English so fluently?
Before you died, neither you nor I
had ever heard an English word.
How did you know
I understood what you said?

I am advised to be careful,
for an old crone can be willful.
Someone guessed you came to fetch me,
as you must feel lonely over there.
Someone asked whether you touched me
or called me by my nickname.
If you did, my number would be fixed.

I'm not scared, nor am I prepared.
If there is another world from where
no one returns, how did you learn
English so well? How come
you drank coffee and ginger ale?
No, no, you couldn't pick up
foreign stuff over there.
You must have been here,
here, in me.

I Woke Up—Smiling

to L. Y.

I was told that I was a sad man.
Sadness is a fatal disease in this place
where happiness is a key to success.
If you are sad, you are doomed to fail—
you can't please your boss,
your long face won't attract customers,
a few sighs are enough
to let your friends down.

Yesterday afternoon I met Pham,
a Vietnamese man who was once a general.
He came to this country
after nine years' imprisonment.
Now he works hard as a custodian
and always avoids
meeting his former soldiers here,
because every one of them
is doing better than he is.
"Sadness," he told me,
"is a luxury for me.
I have no time for it.
If I feel sad
I won't be able to support my family."

Don't dwell on the negative aspects of life → happiness ≠ success

His words filled me with shame,
although I learned long ago
a busy bee feels no sorrow.
He made me realize I'm still a fortunate one
and ought to be happy and grateful
for having food in my stomach
and books to read.

He had no reason not to be happy → his basic needs were getting met.

I returned home humming a cheerful tune.
My wife smiled wondering
why I had suddenly become lighthearted.
My son followed me, laughing and frolicking,
while I was capering on the floor.

his happiness had a pos. impact on his family

13

Last night
I went to a party in my dream.
Voices and laughter were drifting in a large hall
that was full of paintings and calligraphy.
Strolling with ease
I ran into the handwriting of yours
hung in the air
piece by piece waving like wings.
Dumbfounded, I turned
and saw you sitting on a chair,
motionless, the same lean detached face,
only your blue clothes had grown darker.
Something snapped in my chest
and my tears flowed.
What's the use of promising?
I have promised, a hundred times,
but never returned. Wherever we go
our cause is the same:
to make a living and raise children.
If a poem arises, it's merely
an accidental blessing.

For several hours my heart ached,
but I woke up—smiling.

My Mother Also Ate

for Joey Wolenski

They all praised me for being a good boy.
Each by turn asked for a cherry
from the bowl I carried in my hands.
Mother didn't. She was darning my socks.

"Can I have another big one?" Uncle smiled.
I gave him a medium one instead.
Grandpa only had his front teeth left—
his face stretched and contracted as he chewed.
Auntie was holding hers between her lips.
"It's so sweet." She took it out
and put it back into my bowl.

"Why don't you give your mom a cherry?"
Grandpa asked, pointing his pipe at my head.
"Mom doesn't eat good things," I said.

"Why? Doesn't she have a mouth?
Doesn't she know cherries taste good?
Stupid boy, your mom doesn't eat
because she wants to save them for you."

I dropped the bowl and began to cry.
Cherries were sprinkled on the ground.

The Peach

Father, do you remember the peach tree
before our home in the Russian barracks?

It bloomed by the purple paling,
its leaves opened like scissors
in the breeze ringing with bees.

I was three, in a green bib,
eager to pick the peach as big
as a ping-pong ball, the only one
I saw on the tree.

You were weeding with my little spade.
You told me to wait.
"In two months it'll be juicy
and sweet," you assured me.

Every weekend back from the kindergarten
I'd watch my peach. It turned
pink like a bashful face,
bigger and rounder week by week.

Then, one morning I found my peach
half eaten by worms or birds.
A valley was gouged in its belly,
the rotten wound gaping at me.
I didn't cry or say a word.

Father, have you forgotten the peach?
It was my first fruit on a branch.

They Come

I Sing of an Old Land

I sing of an old land
where the gods have taken shelter underground,
where the human idols eat human sacrifice,
where hatred runs the business of philanthropy,
where blazing dragons eclipse the wronged ghosts,
where silence and smiles are the trace of wisdom,
where words imitate spears and swords,
where truth is always a bloody legend.

I speak of the old land not
out of love or wonderment.
Like my ancestors who were scattered into the smoky winds,
who scrambled to leave home
or rushed towards the approaching enemies,
I join those who fled and returned,
        who disappeared in other lands
bearing no hope but persistence, no honor but the story,
        no fortune but parents and children,
singing a timeless curse,
a curse that has bound us together
and rooted us deep in the wreck
        of our homeland.

I touch the land at night—
My hands trace the map on the wall,
from mountains to villages and to rivers,
from plains to cities and to seashores.
I see the green fields of the South,
the dark soil and birch woods of the North,
and snow swirling in summer.

I dream of myself in that land,
not for happiness or harvest.
I dream of suffering together with my people,
of being understood and useful,
of being left alone and able to sleep,
of my children refusing my land

so they will not repeat my life,
of talking and walking with friends,
of completing the work and dying with ease.

I weep for the old land,
for its vast narrowness,
for its profound stupidity,
for its chaos and tenacity,
for its power to possess those of my kind
to devour us to nourish itself
to seize our hearts and throats
and mix our moans with songs—

songs of monstrous grandeur
and merciless devotion,
songs crazed by the cycle of that land.

On a Pottery Figure of a Storyteller from the Eastern Han Dynasty (A.D. 25-220)

The horn on your skullcap wriggles to the beat
from the small drum in your hands. Furrows
of wrinkles wave from your forehead to your ears.
Your eyes are squeezed toward the pointed nose,
beneath which a mouth curves into a slant groove—
words flow out and your trousers get loose
revealing half the raised rump, around which
a cloth band secures a naked paunch
swaying with your bent knees and bare feet.

Why should you complain about your life?
Like Master Homer's, your role
is also to serve and to please.

A Child's Nature

He was to arrive at San Fransisco,
a six-year-old flying from China alone
for twenty hours. We went there to meet him,
hoping he still remembered his parents
now that he had not seen us for three years.

We waited patiently at the airport,
till all passengers came through the customs.
Did he miss the plane?
Why hasn't he shown up? We asked
the clerks of the airline and got no answer.
His mother complained we shouldn't have
let him take such a risk, although she also knew
it was more risky to have him wait until
we could go back and bring him over ourselves.

At last two stewardesses brought him out,
one holding his small suitcase
and the other his hand and his papers.
His mother rushed to carry him up,
kissing and fondling while I was showing
my passport and driver's license to the women,
who said he had been fine but a little frightened.

He still knew his mother but had to be told
I was his father. He looked shy as though
being introduced to a bigger friend.

But he refused to return to the hotel with us.
He said his uncles, aunts, and cousins
were all waiting at the Shanghai airport,
waiting for him to bring back his parents.
After joining us, the whole family would take
a train back to Manchuria. They told him
they had bought eight tickets.

I assured him we would do that after
we saw giraffes in a zoo in San Francisco
and watched whales in another city called Boston.
It didn't matter to stay for a few days.

He told us things in Beijing were in a muddle
when he had been there for the visa with his uncle:
"Lots, lots of hooligans killed soldiers.
There was a counter-revolutionary fight!"

I couldn't believe my ears and asked:
"How come it was 'a counter-revolutionary fight'?
Only the soldiers had guns and tanks
and they killed people on the streets."

"No! Hooligans killed soldiers.
I saw them rob shops on TV.
Lots of trucks were smashed and set on fire.
Grandpa said those were bad eggs
and they wanted to overthrow the government."

"Tantan," his mother said,
"Dad is right. The TV told lies.
Grandpa doesn't know the truth.
The People's Army has changed—
they killed people like us."

We fell into silence
and he looked a little cross.

In the hotel I found a copy of *The Times*
and showed him pictures:
human bodies and bicycles crushed by a tank,
a wounded student being rushed somewhere on a tricycle,
a middle-aged man's face smashed by a gun butt,
a mother crying wildly over the body of her child,
a soldier, naked but with his helmet on,
hanged on the window frame of a wrecked bus.
I pointed at the soldier:
"He killed five innocent people
and was caught when he ran out of bullets.

That's why he was hanged like a pig.
Don't you think he deserved it?"

"No." He shook his head.

"Why not?" I thought he was
beyond hope and couldn't be convinced
by pictures and words.

"Even for that
people shouldn't kill each other."

He kept his voice low
and dared not raise his head.
I was shocked and didn't know what to say.

That night, when he was sound asleep,
I talked to his mother. "Sooner or later
we will return. Cast into Chinese
we are too old to become American.
But Tantan must never go back.
He has too kind a nature
and could not survive there."

July 1989

They Come

Sometimes when you're walking in the street,
returning home or leaving to see a friend,
they come. They emerge from behind pillars and trees
approaching you like a pack hounding a sheep.
You know it's no use to hide or flee,
so you stop and light a cigarette, waiting for them.

Sometimes when you're eating in a restaurant,
your soup served and your dish not ready yet,
they come. A steady hand falls upon your shoulder.
You are familiar with such a hand
and don't need to turn around to meet the face.
The scared diners are sneaking out,
the waitress's chin is trembling when she speaks,
but you are sitting there waiting for the bill.
After settling it you'll walk out with them.

Sometimes when you open your office,
planning to finish an article in three hours,
or read a review, but first make some tea,
they come. They spring out from behind the door
like ghosts welcoming a child to their lair.
You don't want to enter, seeing cups and paper on the floor.
You are figuring how to send a message home.

Sometimes when you have worked day and night,
dog tired, and want to have a good sleep
after a shower and an extra nightcap,
they come. They change the color of your dream:
you moan for the wounds on your body,
you weep for the fates of others.
Only now you dare to fight back with your hands,
but a "bang" or an "ouch"
brings you back to silence and sleeplessness again.

See, they come.

June 1989

to a poet in China

You were arrested last night in my dream.
Your wife fled to her parents in the country
carrying your baby, who was asleep
with his small mouth carelessly open.
Your last words were very simple:
"If I don't come back, remember,
I did nothing but tell the truth."

I cried and started shooting.
My rifle spoke elegantly
splitting every lie in half,
blowing out all the false charges,
quenching the eyes of the police
who struck your cheeks
while handcuffing you.

Since June third
my dreams have run wild,
craving to kill the killers
as if their lives were no more than flies.

In the foreign land
we all watched it unfolding:
the capital was darkened
by a red, red night.

On television I saw
a truck of soldiers pass by and shoot
three men who were watching them move out.
A small girl hid in a rickshaw,
but thirty-nine bullets smashed
the vehicle and the life inside.
Behind her stood a placard:
People are no longer afraid of death,
why do you threaten us with death!
Some blocks away
a young man stopped eighteen tanks
with two bags of groceries.

Here, our flags, our national flags,
have dropped halfway on every pole.
Even schoolchildren stand silent before class.
The whole world knows, except
the Chinese who mourn and celebrate,
mourning for the deaths of murderers,
celebrating the murder of themselves.

History, my friend, is being revised,
just as the blood was scrubbed off
or covered up with grass and flowers,
and the bodies burned to a riddle of numbers.
The killers improvise reasons for killing
while the victims commit a crime
if they are killed.

Everyone says, "Nobody expected
such an end!" An end?
Who knows when it will end?
From fresh stumps hidden in sleeves
deadly hands are growing.
From curses behind doors, from groans in dreams,
an eyeless typhoon is gathering.

June 1989

A Former Provincial Governor Tells About His Dismissal

My dear son, I am pleased to hear
you have passed your qualification.
In the heat of misfortune
you sent me the consolation
that feels like a breeze from the sea.
Thank you, my good son.

You may have heard of my dismissal.
Whatever the newspapers have said,
please ignore it. How could
I take bribes from foreigners
and pocket the education funds?
It was somebody in my office
who used the money to buy a Benz for my use.
I didn't suspect anything when it was done,
but now I'm wondering whether it was a trick
played on me or that man just
wanted to serve me well. Anyway
it's unfair to name me as the chief fraud.

The truth is: after the "Beijing Riot"
I went to the capital in late June.
Before I left, your mother and sister
and my friends all warned me not to go.
They said everybody there
was running away, why was I so eager
to explore the tigers' den.
But I felt I must go and find out the facts,
for we had received a lot of orders
and most of them were in conflict.
Only after knowing what had happened
and what was going on, could we
decide what to follow and with whom to side.

In Beijing I was astounded. I didn't
expect the Government was so stupid

and "the Gang of Old Men" so ruthless—
they dared send in field armies
to kill civilians!
I was upset but kept my mouth shut.

One evening, Chang Sheng invited me
to his home to have a drink.
You know your "Uncle Chang" had been
my bosom friend for thirty years
and his home was as our own.

Three cups loosened my tongue,
but I didn't lose my mind.
I just wanted to speak up, unable to
contain myself any more. Besides,
Chang was one of my sworn brothers.
It was safe without others.

I said those above were fools and thugs
who had ruined the Party and the country
in one night. Why couldn't they have talked
with the demonstrators? Why did they
have to pull in tanks to crush the people
who didn't have an inch of iron in their hands?
You don't shoot a sparrow with artillery.
Now the Party has lost the people's trust
simply because a few old urchins were scared,
so they tore the nation up
to keep their skin unscratched.

I cried and Chang Sheng sighed too.
I knocked my pipe and said loudly:
"Mao Zedong made many mistakes in his life,
but his biggest mistake was
not to have Deng Dwarf finished!"
Chang Sheng smiled and agreed.
We clinked glasses and drank up.

Two days later I was under house arrest.
Mr. Chang sold me to show his loyalty to
his boss. I was told to confess

and make self-criticism, which I refused.
They kept me in an army hospital as though
I had fallen ill. But a week later
I had a heart attack. Probably
they were afraid if I died in Beijing
they would have trouble clearing themselves,
and they knew I had many "brothers,"
so they sent me back for a "home rest."

That is why I was dismissed.
Four days ago Mr. Chang was promoted
to the Party Central Committee
as the head of the Personnel Department.
You wait and see, he will ascend further
to the gallows together with those old men.

My son, don't think my official life
has ended. Those in power won't stay long,
sooner or later we will come back.
A meaningful life is never smooth.
Only in ups and downs is a hero's nature
displayed, only through misfortunes
can we tell who we can trust.
Now I feel good and have time for myself.
I study hard to learn about
the science of governmental affairs.

My son, don't plan to come back soon
or live in America for good.
Study hard and obtain more experience.
Don't waste your time with those there
who only talk of empty democratic theories.
A billion people must be fed.
An impoverished country must be developed.
Only we Chinese ourselves can solve
these problems. The country needs
not those who can only shout slogans
but those who know sciences and have skills.
Whatever happens, please remember
our country's future depends on you,
so you will never get lost.

When it's time to come home
I will let you know.

Words of Your Father
September 4, 1989.

An Escape

The distress of
having to leave &
struggle in a new
country.

We sat in the neon light
on a cool evening of a summer day
drinking beer and eating salad.
You told me your story
similar to those of many others:
All your savings are gone,
the managers, the secretaries, the supervisors,
the police in charge of passports
all having received a handsome share.
Now you have nothing left there,
your color TV and refrigerator were sold
to get the cash for the plane ticket.

"But I was lucky," you assured me.
"Many people have spent fortunes
and still cannot leave the country."

"What are you going to do here?
Don't think this is a place where
you can make a fortune by snapping fingers.
Starting poor, we have to labor for every dollar.
It is a place where money
can hire the devil to make bean curd
and your growth is measured by financial figures.
There is no way for us to get beyond
a social security number."

"Anything, I would do anything,
as long as I can make a living.
At least, I am free here and don't
hate others. Do you know what I wanted
when I was back there?
I always imagined how to get a gun
so I could shoot all the bastards.
That country is not a place to live—
I would die rather than go back."

We stopped to watch seagulls.
An airplane was writing the word
FUN in the distant sky.
I wish I had left the same way,
but I brought with me all my belongings,
even my army mug and a bunch of old letters.

The Fight

I like your cutting at me with a wooden sword
and boasting, "I'm big now, Mom. I can beat Dad!"

With one hand I could raise you in the air,
and break your sword with the other hand.
Or I could pull off your pants and spank you
till you cry and surrender, begging,
"No more. You won. I won't do it again!"
Or my hands could slip under your shirt,
tickle you till you laugh and cough
and collapse on the floor, admitting,
"I'm wrong. I'll be a good boy!"

But for your future I am wielding
a one-foot ruler to parry your strokes.
Whenever hit, I cover the wound with my hand
and my wail brings out your hearty laughter.
Every battle you end up the victor.

To grow is to learn how to *fight back*.
I am your teacher, your rival,
the one doomed to be wrecked.

Bargain

On his first weekend in America
I hired him as a watchman.
Though he was six
he wanted to make some money.

I told him, "There are twelve keys
at different places in this factory.
Every hour I go through them all.
See this clock? I carry it
and punch it at each place.
They pay me seven dollars an hour
and I'll give you three
if you make a round for me.

"It's a good bargain, isn't it?
When I served in the Chinese army
I made six yuan a month. How much
is that in American money?—
just a dollar.

"Now in one day you can make
more than I did in a year.
Don't be scared.
I will go with you."

He was happy
capering ahead with the clock
as we passed the quiet machines.

In a Moonlit Night

Tonight heavy dew disabled mosquitos
that have landed with drenched wings.
Lying on a deck chair on the grass
I watch stars flickering—a luxury,
which I forget I can easily afford.

Fireflies are flitting on the treetops,
katydids chirring in a shaky voice.
A nut or a fruit drops now and then
capering through leaves and twigs.
In the dark a raccoon is lingering,
whose footfalls are timid but never stop.

So large and white is the moon
it reminds me of a huge cake
awaited by hundreds of children
week after week till finally
the Moon Festival came.
Grapes, melons, cherries, crab apples,
nuts, so much food piled on tables.
Every year we skipped lunch in secret
to save our stomachs for the night feast—
eating while watching the harvest moon
and listening to the legends of astral creatures.
Some boys, overstuffed,
would throw up in the small hours.

In Massachusetts tonight
I'm thinking of an old man
who had a bony face and a degree from MIT,
a man we paraded through the streets
and forced to kneel on a platform
because he claimed the American moon
was larger and brighter than the Chinese moon.

How amazed I am to see he was not wrong.
But he couldn't make us believe

there were two moons in the world.
He was silly to use the hated words.
Perhaps he should have explained:
the air here is fresher
and the sky more transparent,
so the moon looks larger and brighter.

No, that won't do.
The implications are still enormous.
He couldn't avoid eating a cowpat.

Gratitude

at an MLA convention

I thought finding a job shouldn't be a problem.
With a doctorate I would have a dozen interviews
and a few offers, like my African friend Patrice
who had four choices and chose a major university.
If so, I promised, I would write a poem
to express my gratitude and must not
attribute the luck to my talent.
Before my eyes emerge thousands
of Chinese coolies shoveling along
the railroad across the American continent.
Their sweaty faces waver in snowflakes,
their breaths and clothes full of
soy sauce and tobacco. At night
they huddle in shanties numbing their pains
with opium and talking about how to ship
the bodies of their fellow men to the homeland.
Ah, I cried, the poem must end with these lines:
"They suffered and perished for the fortune
of their children, and also for mine."

No, nothing has happened as I fancied.
What I have is one interview, but no offer.
My peers are more successful
and some become professorial.
My wife prays for me every night
and even claims she will believe in God
if her husband finds a job. Good-for-nothing,
the feeling of uselessness is the supreme humility.

These days
many lines and stories come to mind.
I remembered the fate of Tu Fu and Li Po—
two great poets who had the bitterest lives.
The Lord of Heaven wanted them to sing,
so he made them feed on misfortune.
He cut their wings and put them into cages
and forced them to watch other birds soaring.

I said to myself: This must be another trick
Heaven plays on you, to make your words come
not from a sore throat but from a twinging belly.
All right, for this I am grateful. At least
Heaven groups me with those chosen to be poets.

Those ancient masters were also forced to leave home.
They wandered through barbarous lands
fleeing the flames of war or refusing to serve
a lord other than their own. A few managed
to return, but to a home of weeds and graves
or to a village where no one
was old enough to remember their faces.
Those ancients had no shame of tears—
missing home, they cried at any gathering.
Their friends joined them in weeping,
pipes and strings yanking everyone's guts,
while sorrowful songs were improvised.
Their bitterness was tasted from mouth to mouth
through thousands of years.

No matter how we feel, we must not weep,
for tears are cheap and do not please.
Home can be anywhere but the place
our dreams fly to. It is a sinking boat
that everyone strives to leave.
Only weaklings have to eat the grain
that feeds on the bones and ashes of our ancestors.
Our bodies can enrich the soil
of any land.

How brazen I was
to link myself to those unyielding ancients.
My gratitude to Heaven was mere arrogance.
Compared with them, I am fortunate,
for my family is sheltered and we do not starve,
and I can even afford to stay in a hotel
where a thousand lectures are delivered in two days,
where professors look awesome as speakers and hirers.
Yet, do not mention again the beauty of this free land.
Freedom here is not a way of living

but a way of selling and buying. To survive
one has to learn how to sell oneself
and how to trim oneself into a bolt or a nut
to match the machine of a profession.
Still, I cannot but feel grateful
for being allowed to stay or go,
for knowing one price of freedom.

At Midnight

At Midnight

Suddenly ducks and geese were clamoring.
On the lake the shadows of a street lamp
were shattered by wings exploding.
Startled, she went
to drop the window curtain.

"My God, so many of them," a man cried.
He was feeding them, his dog barking.

She stopped to watch
the water swashing and sparkling.

Her cat jumped into her arms.

Astrological Signs and Marriage

Two dogs shouldn't share a roof.
They will bark and bite
till one turns tail or bites the dust.
A cow must avoid a mouse
that can enter her stomach
through either nostril.
A rabbit mustn't nestle with a snake—
a little dragon—that will kill
without second thoughts.

He's a monkey while I'm a sheep.
The fortune-teller said:
the sheep had a good temperament
eating grass and giving milk;
in contrast, the monkey had brains,
a capable shepherd by nature,
so we were a well-matched couple.

We've been married for a year
and I'm sick of his "shepherding."
He rides on me night and day,
sucking my nipples whenever he's hungry.
His mother told their neighbors,
"A sheep is a monkey's cow."

On Receiving a Calendar

My friend sent me a calendar
full of dogs—a red wolf,
a white leopard, a mottled fox,
all painted by G. Castiglione,
an Italian monk who went to Peking
two hundred years ago
and became a master painter
at the Imperial Court.

Picture by picture
it sings of the Dog Year
and the distant wish
for health, fortune, and peace.

To me alone it sings of a town
and the laughter of a "queen,"
who remains to me as a beautiful dog.
It also sings of the dwellings
I promised her when we played house:
a villa, a palace, a temple,
a skyscraper, a castle...

though she often called me names
for the rickety house
I built for her German shepherd.

Summer Grass

Yesterday afternoon my son asked,
"What does 'middle-aged' mean, Dad?"
I said, "Neither young nor old."

"Just like you?" He looked up at me
and put down his *Andersen's Tales*
on the summer grass. I nodded
but wondered whether I had to agree.

His question surprised me.
That was the first time
I accepted myself as middle-aged,
although I checked dictionaries
that all say middle age begins at forty.

You once declared you couldn't bear
being loved by a younger man.
I was hopeless and unqualified.
If you saw me now you would be impressed
by how much I have advanced.
Last month on the town green
an old lady even wanted to know
whether my wife was a daughter of mine.

At last I feel very qualified,
for the same passion no longer
tightens my chest or spins my head.
It is so easy for me to improvise a jest
and take everything with two minds.

Nowhere can you find the old cry
except in these simple lines—
my words are still my palms and fingers.

If You Had Not Thrown Me Away

If you had not thrown me away
I would have forgotten you,
just as many girls' faces appear in my mind
but no matter how hard I try
I cannot remember their names.
Those eyes like spring water,
those voices like silver bells,
those lips like roses
have all grown bleary
in my memory and mingled
with bus tickets, bills, and syllabi.
How often I tap my forehead and swear,
"Damn it, my brain has been churned
into a bucket of paste!"

I cannot imagine how you look now,
how you go to a grain shop to buy rice,
how you get to kindergarten immediately after work,
how you quarrel with your husband,
how you become the "manager" of a family.

What recurs most is your dancing skirt
that used to be a colorful UFO
carrying my heart to the blue sky.

If you had not thrown me down to the earth
how could I lie watching the white clouds for so long,
now lowering my head smiling,
now repeating your secret name?

Before Dawn

Stars have sunk beyond the autumn çlouds.
Once more my thoughts drift
through the frosty winds
to a town covered with red roofs.
Sleepy birds quack and shriek
from the shadowy woods
announcing momentary surrender
or rapturous conquest.

They call up love—
my love for a woman sick of love
and for a country demanding more than love.
Both dazzled me with their beauty
that was a vision
cast by my innocent eyes.
Now they are convinced
that choked with hate and malice
I fled to this place,
in exotic solitude
attending a swollen ego.

How could they conceive
that all these years
I have crept through pages
wriggling in word-irons
only to prove that
I am a competent lover
who, not praising,
may still produce pride?

Distance

Your voice is so young
it led me to a younger generation.

Yesterday I played many times
your nameless message
thinking of all the young women
who might have my phone number.
None of them had the childlike voice,
so familiar, yet out of reach.
I don't know this girl, I thought
and didn't call you back.

This morning I woke with your voice
ringing in my head, mingled
with the cuckoo in the birch woods where
we walked together fifteen years ago.
It was in Harbin, in that windy spring.

Suddenly I felt old, tired of
wandering alone in this land.
I called San Francisco
but you had left
with the delegation
of your country.

The Scent of the Sun

On the rim of the bathtub
she left me a towel,
fluffy and folded,
soaked with sunlight.
I buried my face in the nap
to inhale the sun.

In my chest a world is rippling,
a world of seagulls,
fishing boats, tides, hurricanes,
pollen and bees, kids,
bacon, laughter and song.

If someone tells me again,
"The sun smells the same anywhere,"
I will say to him,
"Not in every home."

Nets

War

Back there they gave me a gun
and told me to shoot and stab.
"Put a red flower on their chests.
Let your bayonet go in
and come out wet."
The targets were clear:
Russian Tartars, American wolves,
Japanese devils, Taiwanese bandits.
I fought and fought,
sick and tired.
War was a public compass.

fighting physical enemies

Here I've lived my war
fighting shadows.
No enemy is visible
and no gun useful.
Small supple hands
toting tiny bundles of cash
stroke my throat and pat my hair,
ready to pin me to the ground
and turn me into a happy worm.
A secretive voice rasps,
"Live in the flesh only!"

fighting internal enemies

So I spur my soldier
with songs.

Nets

Yes, life happens in nets.
How I admire those who creep,
eat and sleep in a net with ease,
those who mend or brace a net,
who enjoy watching me
dive into a holey wall
scraped or crippled,
those who thrill
at my tossing and twisting.

If only I could be at home in a net
—that isn't a bad thing.
A net is a shelter at least
and can be a stage
or a hunting zone.

I have fled many nets
but always wandered into another one—
there are nets outside a net
and nets within a net.
I am a frog with useless wings.

An Apology

I also wonder why I said
it would waste my time
to write an autobiography,
although an "I" story
can sell better than poetry
and may fetch a brief name.

Please forgive me.
I didn't mean to chill your birthday
and season the chicken and honeydew
with a tart argument.
Nor did I know you had authored a book
about your girlhood.

Though my words tumble,
my pen can't help
redrawing my circumference.
On paper I dare to laugh
or weep like a free man.
On paper I can reach
for a hand, a face,
a cloud, or thunder.

The "I" ought to be conquered
when we cage stars on the page.

Reverberation

My friend came and spent a weekend here.
In China he used to be an interpreter
and guide foreign mountaineers.

He told me he had once accompanied
a group of Japanese
to a snow mountain in the Uighur Region.

They climbed for a whole day
but did not make the summit.
A storm was gathering, so they turned back.

On their way down, a young woman
(the only one on the team) fell off a cliff
and disappeared in the ice below.

She was injured but not fatally.
"Help, help me!" she yelled
at the men two hundred feet above her.

None of them went down,
though they were all well trained.
They listened and turned on a recorder.

"Help, help! I'll pay you ten million yen!"
Her screams were kept on a cassette tape
for her family and insurance company.

"Those Japs are beasts,"
my friend said. "If she were a Chinese
I would've gone down to help her."

His story saddened me. After he left,
the voice still lingered in my home—
"Help, I'll pay you ten million yen!"

I don't know if he could be so gallant
to a Chinese woman as he claimed.
I've begun to walk my dog every day.

Blessing

I plan to ask an old man for his blessing
at the church where I heard him preaching.
I'm going to tell him:
After many nights' tossing in bed
I have chosen a way of living,
that is, to earn my bread with my pen.

I want to ask the old man for his blessing:
Please bless me and my family.
My wife and children are willing
to go with me to a hazy place.
They know I'm after something
that has led men and women
to fight shadows in a maze.
Oh please bless me, my wife
and my children.

I wait for the old man and his blessing.
At the church I pray for his arrival.
By luck and diligence
I may be worthy of his grace,
making words prance on the page.
I wait and wait and wait,
but no one has come.
Only the wind is blowing—
I bless myself with leaves swirling.

Father

I looked for a father in several men.
One of them used to be a sailor,
sailing to different lands
and now writing novels.
Another is a monastic singer,
whose voice, steely and mellow,
shook me to tears and song.
Another is a thinker, forced to wander,
his thoughts so keen
they pruned my mind like scissors....

I have sent them many letters
but never received an answer.
Still I wondered whether
I should put their names in my résumé.

These days I hear a voice whisper,
"Those men prefer to have daughters.
You'd better father yourself."

On a Giant Pine Tree

Who dropped it here, a bird or a wind?
How many rings are in the trunk?
How far do the roots extend?
Are these stumps needed
for thickening the limbs?
Or are they merely wreckage
left by storms?

Here it stands alone
at the edge of a grassland,
a landmark that itself needs no mark.

Beyond the grass, the lake
is shimmering in the sun.
Geese are floating, still asleep,
their bills buried in their wings;
fish dive and jump
breaking the calm of dawn.

Far away on the other shore
woods are sprawling, millions
of trees tilting toward the horizon.
Together they brave the elements
that can't kill all.

The woods are flourishing,
but every tree is slender
raising a tiny crown.
For air and sun it strives upward
elbowing its neighbors down;
for water and soil
they tussle underground.
The strong grow slowly in circles
while the weak shrink and die.
Yet, what magnitude
their green union shows.

This pine, alone,
gathers more wind,
but it stands large and tall,
its cones hanging like pineapples.

A Revelation

I was forking wheat bundles
in my dream last night
when a horse lumbered over.
He scared me because he had no skin,
his flesh white as cheese.
I patted his flank
which began quivering,
so I stopped to observe him.
His drowsy eye could hardly open,
yet the pupil blinked
showing he knew me, quite well.
He followed me from barn to barn,
then grazed alone in the pasture,
whisking his long tail
at the bluebottles buzzing around.

When spring came, everywhere
catkins were flying.
Among weeping cherries I met him again.
He looked shiny and sturdy
covered with mottled down
like a birdling's.
He seemed happy to see me,
stretched his nose to my arm
and capered about—

Rat-tat, rat-tat-tat,
a woodpecker cracked my dream.

Outside, morning
was flapping its wings.

I rubbed my chest,
ready for another bruise.

In New York City

In the golden rain
I plod along Madison Avenue,
loaded with words.
They are from a page
that shows the insignificance
of a person to a tribe,
just as a hive keeps thriving
while a bee is lost.

On my back the words
are gnawing and gnawing
till they enter into my bones—
I become another man,
alone, wandering,
no longer dreaming of luck
or meeting a friend.

No wisdom shines
like the neon and traffic lights,
but there are words as true as
the money eyes, the yellow cabs,
the fat pigeons on the sills.

The Past

I have supposed my past is a part of myself.
As my shadow appears whenever I'm in the sun
the past cannot be thrown off and its weight
must be borne, or I will become another man.

But I saw someone wall his past into a garden
whose produce is always in fashion.
If you enter his property without permission
he will welcome you with a watchdog or a gun.

I saw someone set up his past as a harbor.
Wherever it sails, his boat is safe—
if a storm comes, he can always head for home.
His voyage is the adventure of a kite.

I saw someone drop his past like trash.
He buried it and shed it altogether.
He has shown me that without the past
one can also move ahead and get somewhere.

Like a shroud my past surrounds me,
but I will cut it and stitch it,
to make good shoes with it,
shoes that fit my feet.

Rock

When I die I wish to be a rock
dropped into a shallow river.
In three months it will be girdled
with moss, its bottom firm in the mud.
Soon fish arrive to store
their eggs in the notches and cracks.
In time baby fish will find holes
and settle beneath the rock.
Then come turtles that love
the shade behind the rocky shoulder
and the taste of ducklings swimming by.
A few snakes sense life in the water,
so they creep over, digging tunnels,
sharpening poison; they climb up
to sun their bellies on the rock—
I don't budge.

To Ah Shu

It's raining in Boston tonight.
The roofs glisten while thunder
rumbles through the spring woods.
Again, I took out your letters
and read them one after another.
Some I had remembered well,
a few I found bear new meanings.

Your last letter arrived two weeks ago.
It made me ill—homesick for some days.
I dreamed of meeting you in Harbin,
where lilacs are blooming and steamboats
are ready to sail down the Sungari to Russia.
We introduce our wives and children,
as they have never spoken to each other,
having met only through photographs.
These days, I think of the dream,
unable to tell when it will come true.

You suggest for the moment
I study Greek and Latin so as to bring
those ancient voices back to China,
where poets have callous ears
listening to voices in our own tongue
through three thousand years.
I agree, I should return.
Hard life is never a problem,
since we Chinese are used to hardship.

What worry me are the political storms
that can arise from a few coughs. Besides,
I'll not be allowed to write or translate.
Who is interested in Homer and Virgil now?
Who dares to publish their works?
The Greeks and the Romans may also
be class enemies. Won't I be accused
of disseminating Western democracy
If I say Achilles challenged Agamemnon?

You are right, in the end it's sacrifice
that makes a difference, but how can we tell
sacrifice from suicide?
(I know, such a question deprives
the questioner of his dignity
and instead reveals his cowardice.)

For Heaven's sake, if only I were
a Christian so my heart didn't have to
embrace a nation—wherever I go
I would serve the same God!

We Chinese do not revere the divine:
we worship the country as our God,
which often runs wild like a dog.
We're supposed to weave our personal grief
into the fortune of the large tribe,
whose strength resides in consuming
every one of us. This is why I feel
so miserable writing in English
which I love but wish not to use,
since we ought to labor in our own tongue,
to keep it from decay and make it great.

I know my cries in this alphabet
will compound my "crimes" and take me further away
from you, my dearest friend. But I have to write
and have to choose between being a good citizen
or a good writer. For the Chinese,
nobility lies in claiming both.
This means to sacrifice one's life
for the integrity of one's words.
Sacrifice, oh sacrifice, it will only end
in the truncation of the meaningful work
that might eventually bring honor to our race.

But I must survive as a writer.
Also, I'm a father and want my child
to live a better life than my own.
Someday I may return. I hope by then
I'll be able still to work and not merely
to be cremated in our homeland.

Like you, I also feel my heart old.
This isn't necessarily bad for a poet.
What's dreadful is to have only juvenile emotions
while one's age has progressed. Most
Chinese writers today have not completed
the transition from youth to middle age:
they have indeed suffered unthinkable misfortunes
but their hearts remain soft and young.
Their voices may be sweet and delicate,
but they seldom convey the weight of reality
or send out the glow of truth and wisdom.

To grow is to obtain an ancient passionate heart,
to write is to liberate words from that heart.
(Tomorrow I'll send you a copy of Yeats.)

As for Milosz, I don't have his new book yet.
I went to hear him read once and was disillusioned,
just as I was at other readings
given by Brodsky, Snyder, and Bly.
Their poetry is fine, but as human beings
they are not so sacred as we imagined.
We've taken many Western poets to be models
or masters, who are actually our own fantasy.
Very often at those gatherings, I feel lonely
finding myself unrelated to what is read.
I prefer to stay home, reading Chekhov,
or writing a letter, or learning a few words.

The rain has stopped and the night
becomes chilly. It's time to wake
my son so that he will not wet his bed.
The peach trees in our yard will surely
bloom tomorrow morning, but
spring means little to me ever since
I've been here. So often echo in my ears
those distant horses' hooves
clattering upon the asphalt road
when we walked under your umbrella in the rain
talking about our youthful aspirations
and that never-finished manifesto.

Lilburn, Georgia

for Sam Hamill

I broke some large stones
and with a hand truck carried them home.
Along the edge of the lake in my yard
I piled them piece by piece
to make the soil stay.

My joy in the labor evoked Tu Fu's line:
"The river flows but stones remain."
I saw him standing on a cliff
lamenting the disappearance of things man-made—
fleets, palaces, cities, empires, fame.
Above, geese are passing,
below, the Yangtze lapping sand.

Time and again
his voice rings among my stones.

In the Small Hours

The moon shines on the maples,
whose shadows darken on the grass
when the night turns silver
ringing with cicadas.

Coby barks,
aroused by a pinecone
that dropped into the pond.

Through the window
moonlight slants in—
a bright octagon on the floor,
a jug of ice crackling...

A serene night,
no matter where,
should give similar joy.